Dedicated to my Mom,
a Brooklyn girl who for unexplained reasons
loved elephants.

Special thanks to Morgan and Diana.

Elephants Make Great House Pets
Text and Pictures Copyright
© 2018 by Mal Karlin

This book my be purchased in bulk for promotional, educational, or business use. Please contact Mal Karlin at 212-779-3375, malkarlin@gmail.com

ISBN- 978-0-692-19405-8
    978-0-692-19413-3

Published by IngramSpark

ELEPHANTS MAKE GREAT HOUSE PETS

Written and Illustrated By Mal Karlin

Elephants make great house pets...

...except for the times when
they need to be walked.

Elephants make great house pets...

...except for the times when
they want to sleep in your bed.

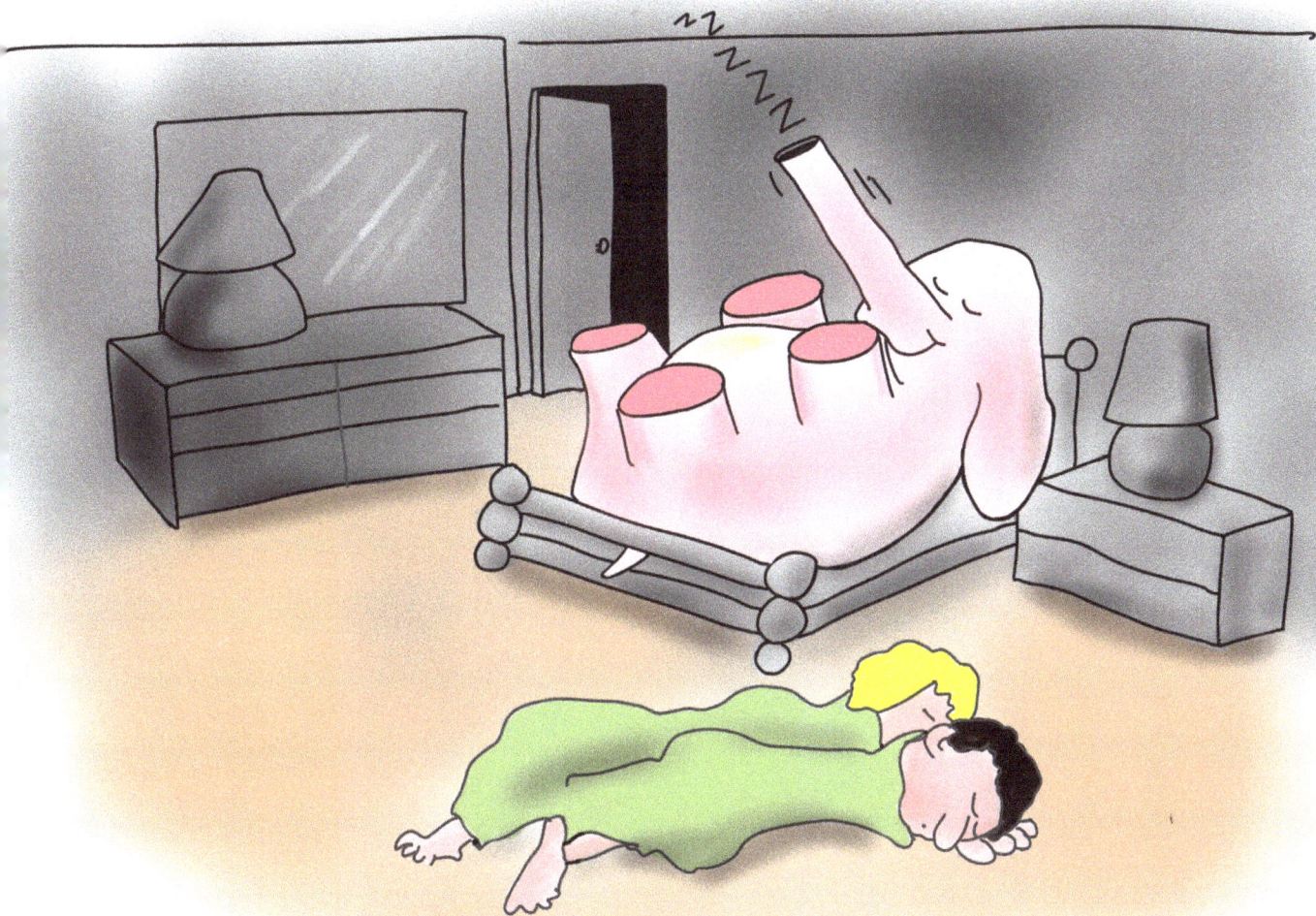

Elephants make great house pets...

...except for the times when
they are looking for affection.

Elephants make great house pets...

...except for the times when
they are hungry for table scraps.

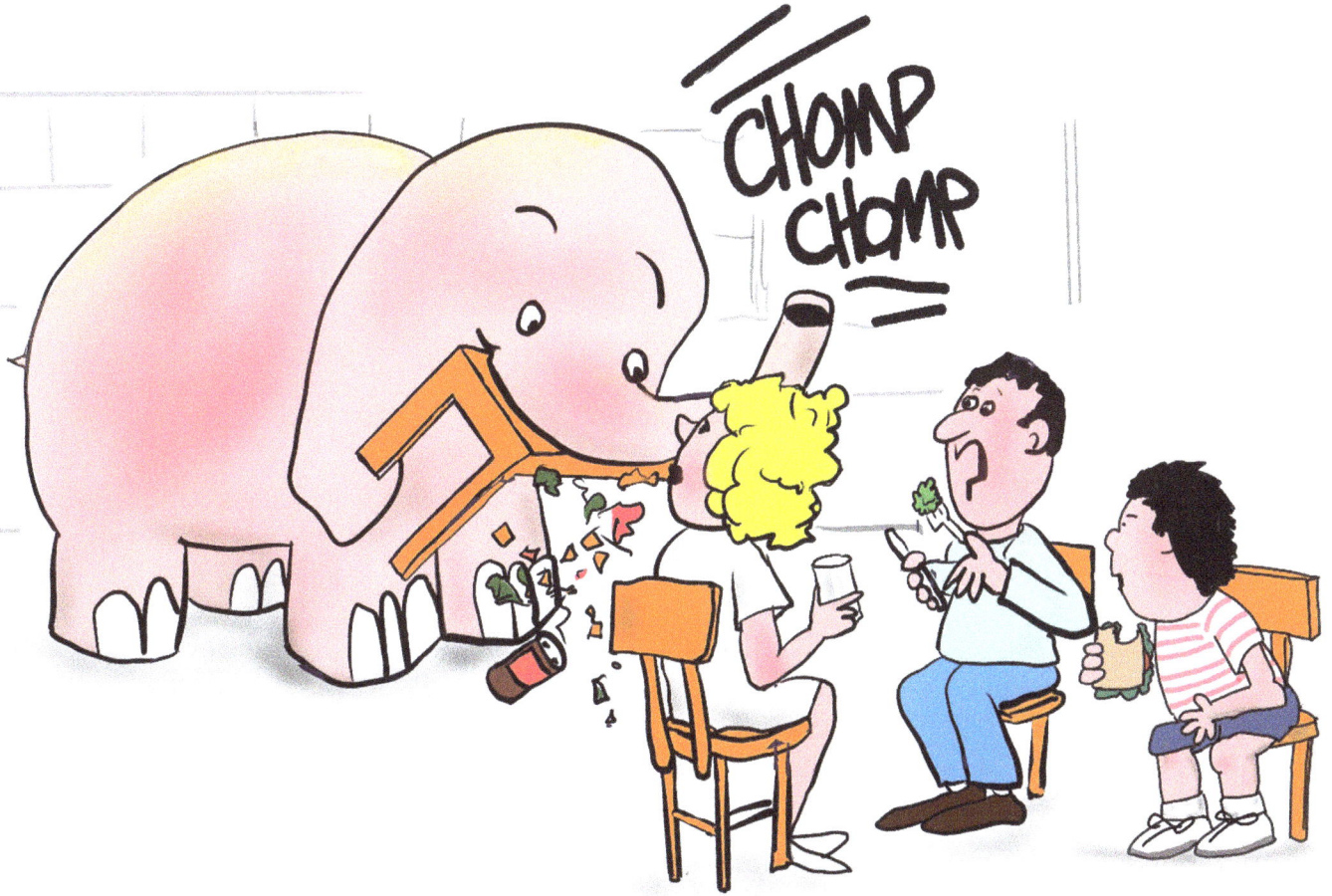

Elephants make great house pets...

...except for the times when
they get scared.

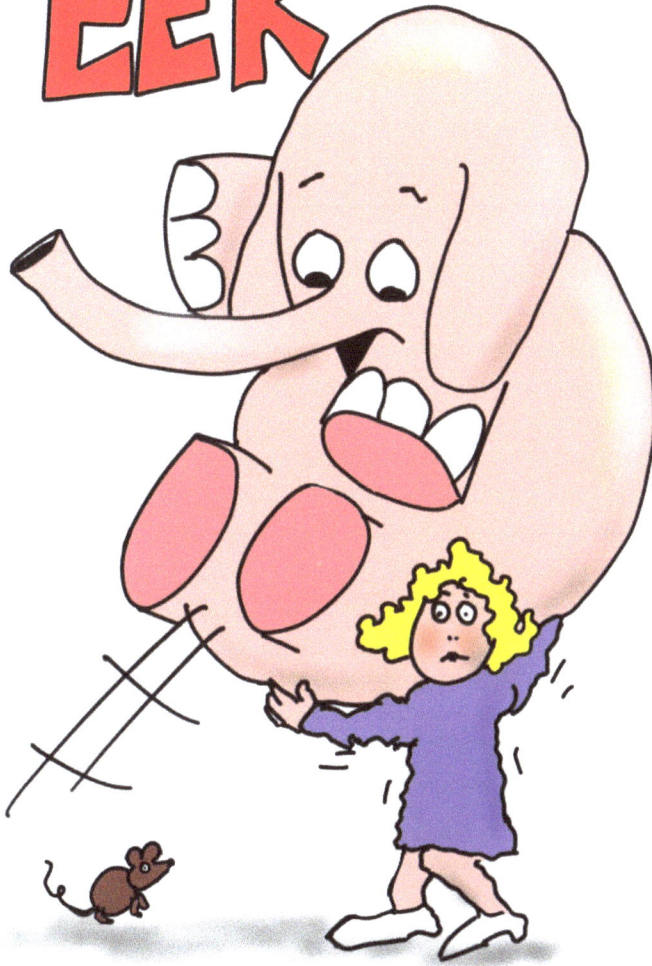

Elephants make great house pets...

...except for the times when
you go on a family picnic.

Elephants make great house pets...

...except for the times when
you play fetch.

Elephants make great house pets...

...except for the times when they make a bathroom mistake in the house.

Elephants make great house pets...

...except for the times when
they catch a cold.

Elephants make great house pets...

...except for the times when
you have to get to the other side of
the room.

Elephants make great house pets...

...except for the times when
you play frisbee in the park.

Elephants make great house pets...

...except for the times when
you give them a bath.

Elephants make great house pets...

...except for the times when
they eat beans for dinner.

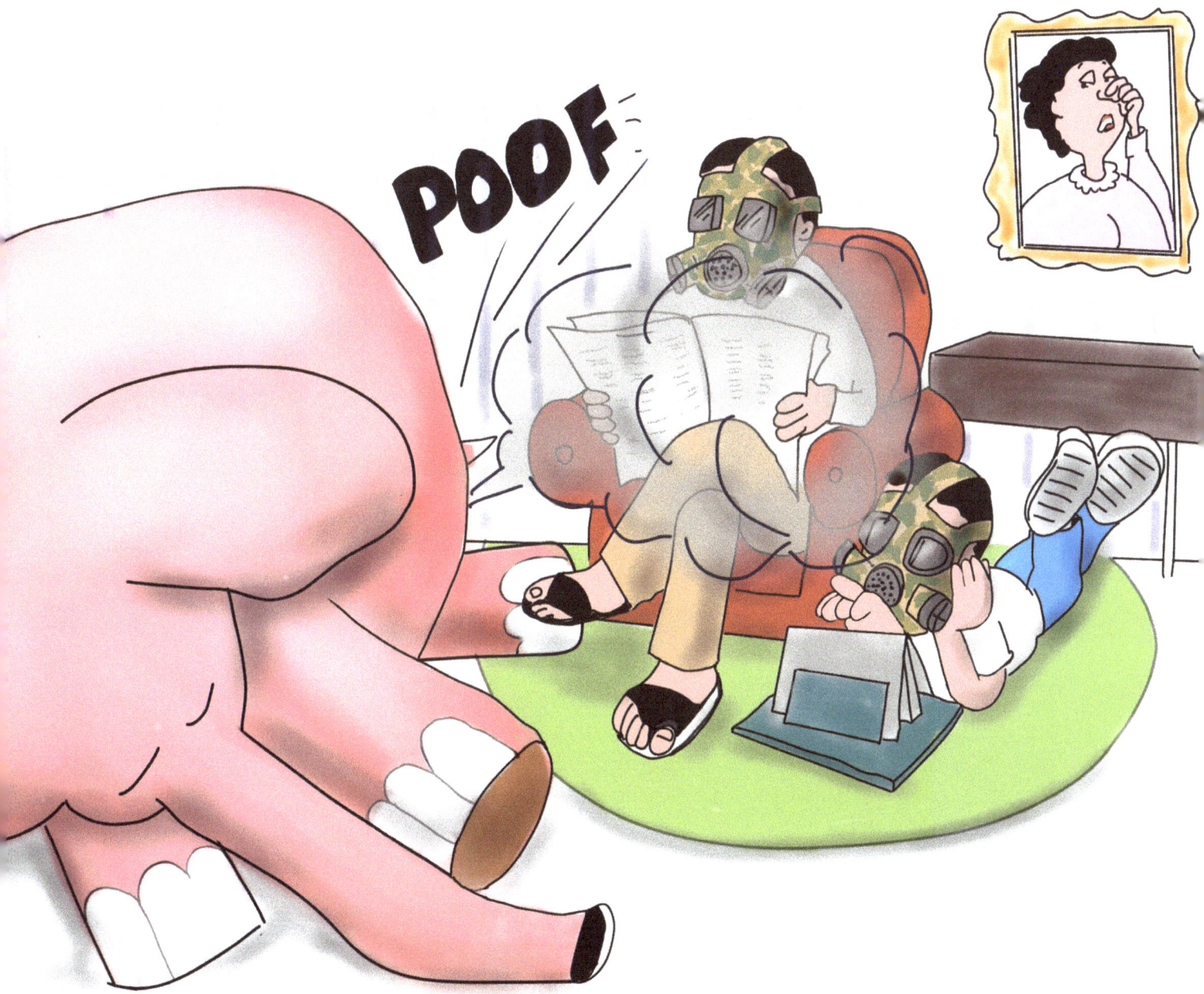

Elephants make great house pets...

...except for the times when you want a drink of water at night.

Elephants make great house pets...

...except for the times when
they want to kiss you.

SMACK

Elephants make great house pets...

...except for the times when your aunt and uncle drop by to visit.

Elephants make great house pets...

...except for the times when their friends come by to play.

Elephants make great house pets...

...especially the times when they make you laugh.

www.ingramcontent.com/pod-product-compliance
Lightning Source LLC
Chambersburg PA
CBHW040249100426
42811CB00011B/1198